So You Want to Learn About

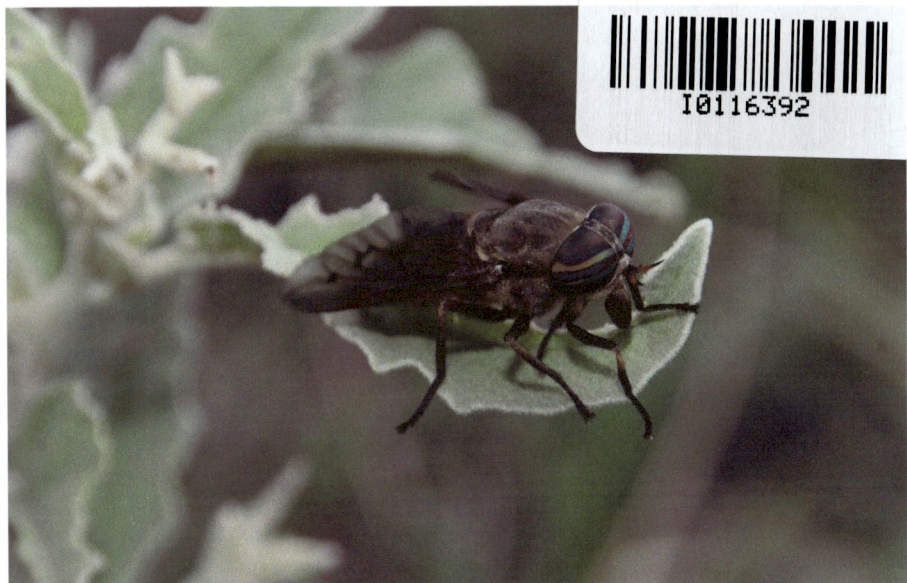

Insects & Bugs

Written and Photographs by
Katrina Willoughby

I hear you want to learn about insects and bugs!

Insects include ants, flies, bees, beetles and more.

Bugs is a broader term that includes insects and other creatures. Typically, a bug is considered to have a beak like mouth. There are lots of creatures that get called bugs.

Insects have 3 segments to their body, a head, thorax and abdomen. On some insect, like the ant below, their segments are easy to see.

All insects have antennae, compound eyes and six jointed legs.

Do you think that a spider is an insect? How many legs does it have?

The answer is that a spider has 8 legs, so it has too many legs to be an insect.

We can still call it a bug.

Insects and bugs don't have bones in their bodies.

Instead they have an exoskeleton; a skeleton on the outside of their body. The exoskeleton provides both protection and support for an insect's muscles. The spider above grew too large for its old exoskeleton. A new one grew and the old one was shed off. The old one can be seen to the left in the picture.

We don't know how many species of insects live on the earth. Over 1.5 million species have been identified and some scientists think that there could be as many as 9 million different species. That is a lot of insects!

There are more than 380,000 species of beetles alone.   Here you can see a beetle know as the fig beetle or green June bug.

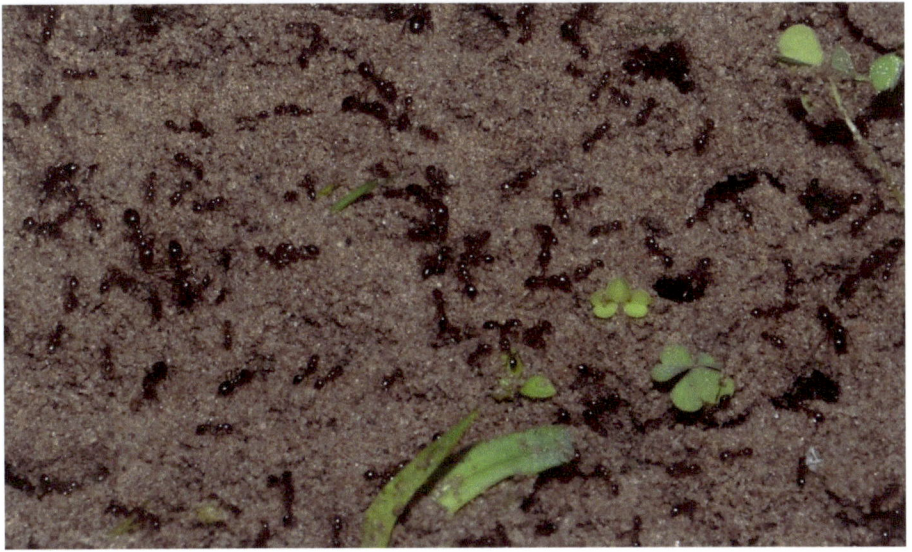

The world's ant population might be 1.4 million times bigger than the human population! Ants live in colonies with many other ants. Here you can see ants in their colonies.

An ant will have a specific role in its colony. For example, it may be a worker ant's job to forage for food, defend the colony, take care of young, or build their home.

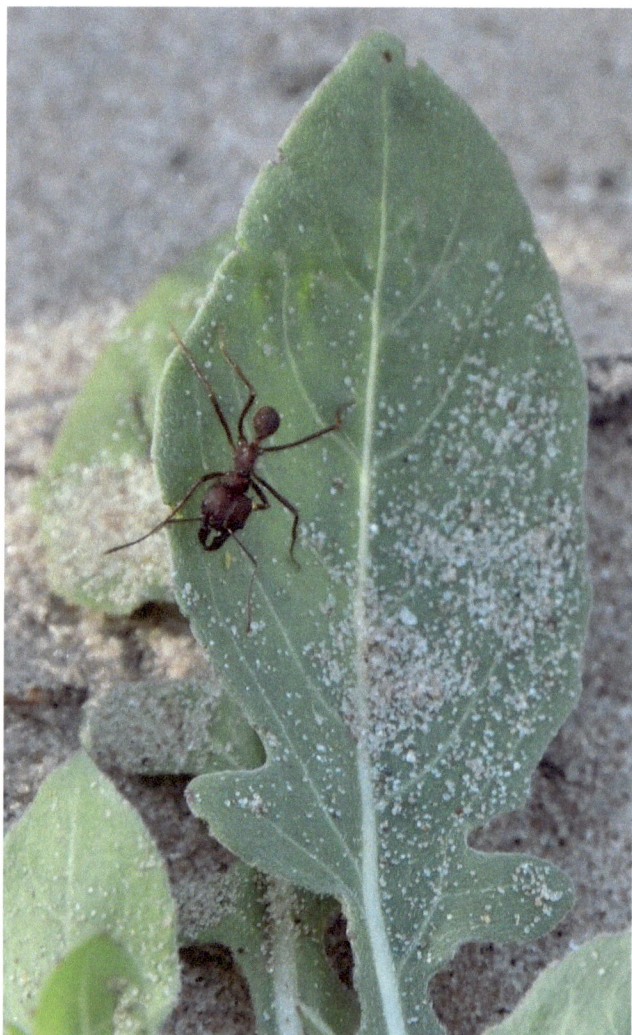

Leaf cutter ants trim off little pieces of leaves and carry them back to the colony where they add them to their 'garden'. These ants are growing fungus for food! This ant is getting ready to cut a piece off of this leaf.

Insects do not breathe through a nose. They use spiracles, holes in the sides of their exoskeleton, to bring in air. Valves on the spiracles open and close to bring air into tubes allowing the insect to breathe.

The spiracles on this is sphinx moth can be seen as dark dots along its abdomen.

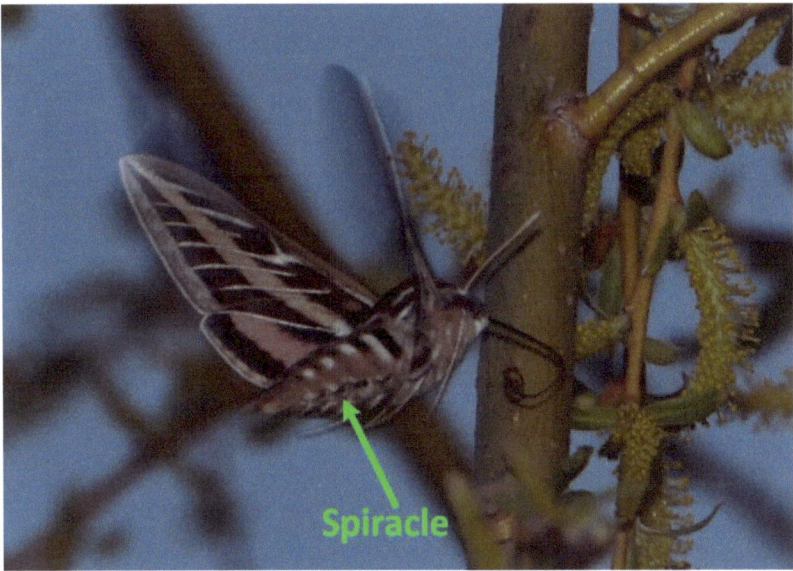

Spiracle

This moth's wings can beat as fast as 80 times per second. It often gets mistaken for a hummingbird and is also known as a hummingbird moth.

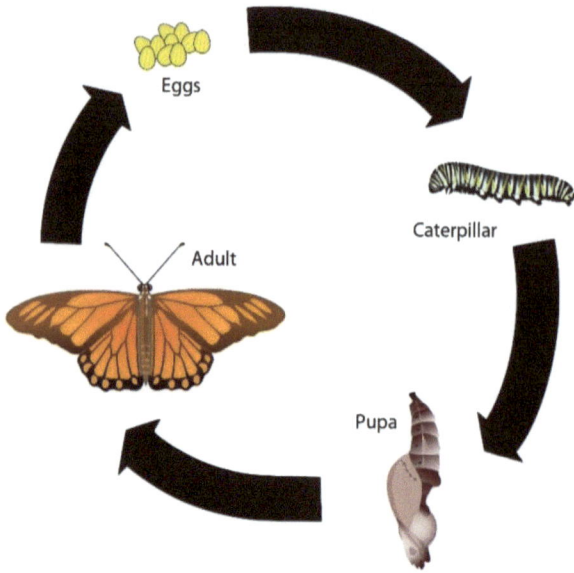

Insects lay eggs. Some insects, like butterflies, will hatch as a caterpillar, form into a pupa, then transform into something very different like a butterfly. This transformation is called metamorphosis. The caterpillar above will eventually turn into a sphinx moth like the one on the previous page.

A June bug will go through the process of

metamorphosis in its life. After eggs are laid, they will hatch into grubs, a type of caterpillar that lives in the ground.

The grub will form into a pupa and stay in the ground until it emerges as a beetle.

The pupa picture here will probably turn into a moth. It was found in the ground.

There are many different species of June bugs across the world.

Other insects don't change quite so much. When they hatch they are called nymphs. They look similar to an adult but will go

through different stages, such as getting wings, as they grow into adults. The life cycle for these insects is called incomplete-metamorphosis.

Insects like the mayfly pictured above, grasshoppers, cockroaches, and dragon flies go through incomplete-metamorphosis.

Dragonflies can fly up to 50 miles per hour.

Humans have blood vessels; insects don't. Their circulatory system works different than ours. Blood flows freely in their bodies without being confined to tubes.

We need bugs in our lives! They are very important in the food chain. They pollinate the crops we eat and other plants. The bee in the previous picture pollinates this flower while collecting pollen. Lots of other animals eat bugs. Bugs help to decompose things like dead trees and leaves. We even get things like honey and silk from bugs!

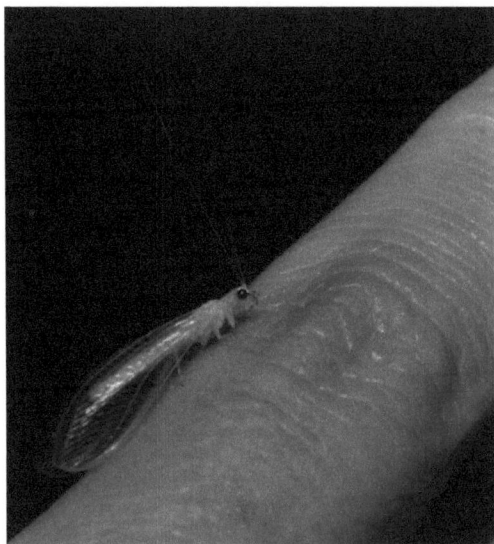

Most bugs are completely harmless to people. Some bugs do bite or eat crops.

Mosquitoes are famous for biting. Only the females bite. The picture to the left is an Asian tiger mosquito. They get the name from black and white stripes on their legs and body.

Unlike mosquitoes, the midge insect doesn't bite. They often get mistaken for mosquitoes but you can tell a male midge because it has fuzzy antennae. Mosquitoes don't have fuzzy antennae.

Unfortunately, some insects can be very bad for crops. Some insects, like locusts, can eat their weight in food in a single day. It takes a human about a year and a half to eat as much as they weigh.

Grasshoppers and locust look alike, but they are different insects.

The blister beetle has been known to devastate crops when large numbers of them show up to eat. There are 2500 different species of blister beetles.

On the right you can see just a few of the many blister beetles that were eating in a farmer's field.

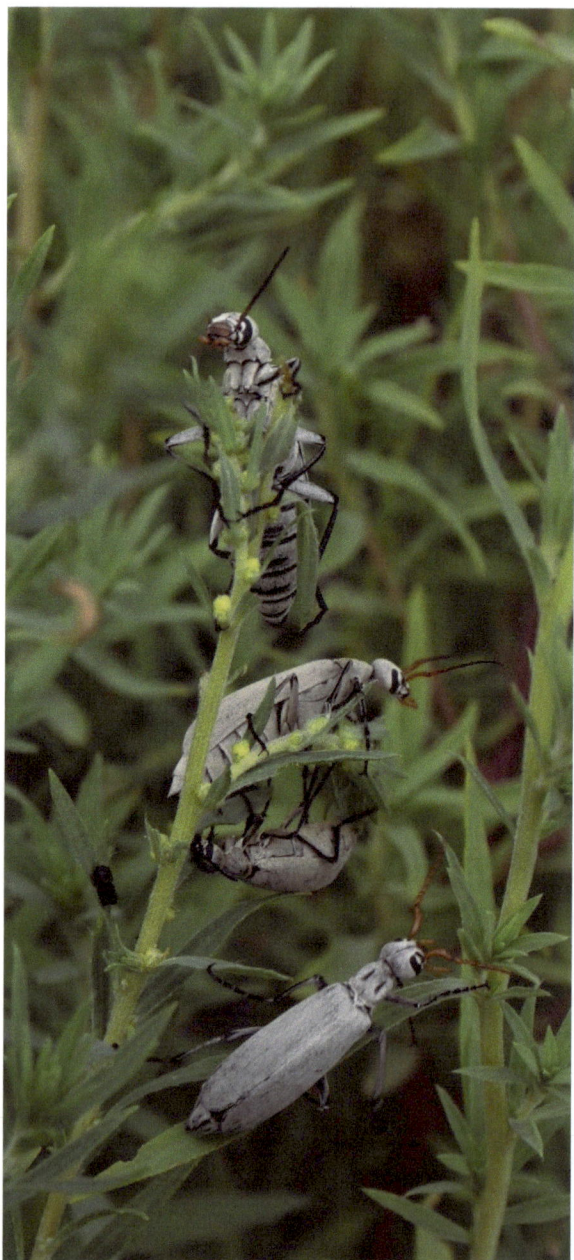

Around 100,000 species of flies have been identified in the world. Most flies live for only a month.

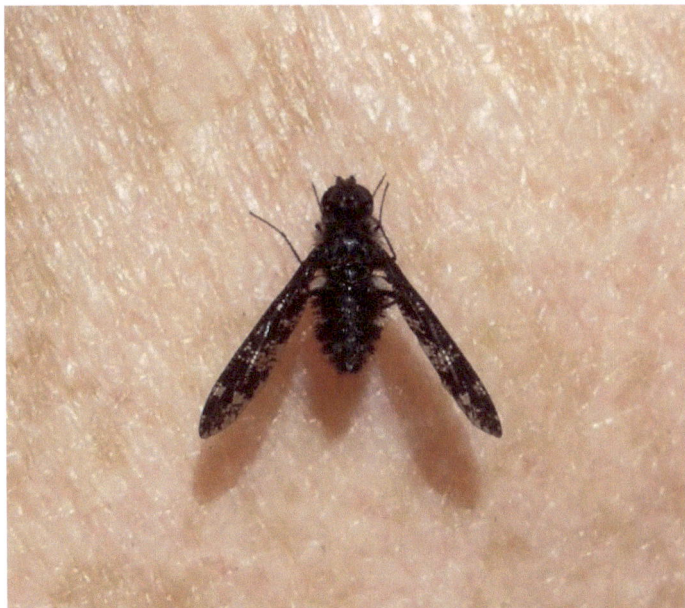

The bodies of flies are covered with things that look like hair.

Can you see the little hairs on this fly?

Deer flies are much bigger then house flies.
They can bite hard. A deer fly is pictured
above. Some of them have extremely
gorgeous eyes! A house fly is below.

Houseflies can't bite you. Their mouth is similar to a butterfly's.

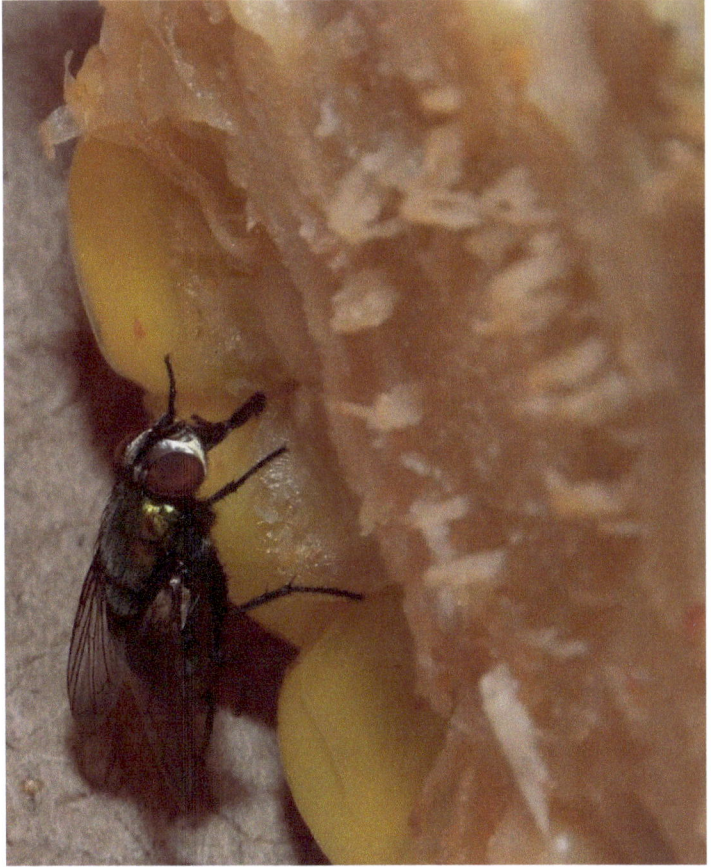

They have a long tube called a proboscis that they drink fluids through. Digestive juices are spit out onto food through a house fly's proboscis. Food gets dissolved so they can drink it up. The fly above is enjoying corn on the cob.

Butterflies dine on food that is ready to be sipped up. This butterfly has its proboscis extended to drink a meal.

The easiest way to tell a butterfly from a moth is to look at its antennae. A butterfly will have smooth antennae while a moth will have furry looking antennae.

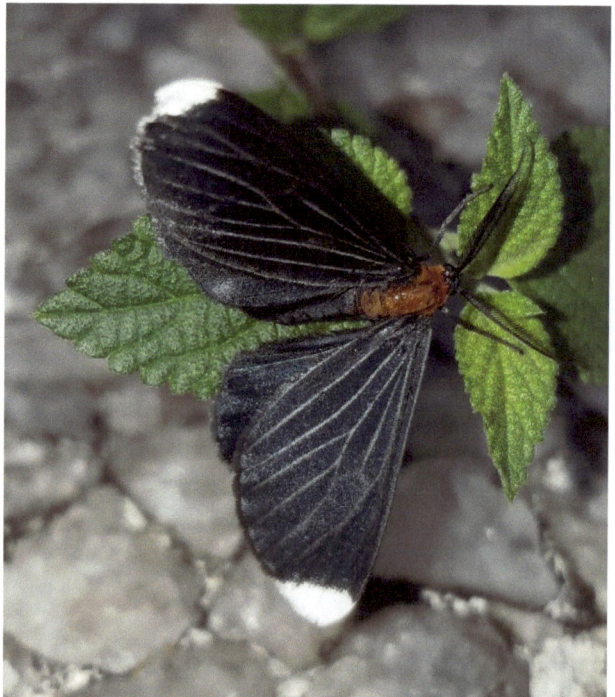

On the previous page it is easy to see the fuzzy antanne on a white-tipped black moth.

This little moth is called a plume moth. While it has a very unique look, it might be mistaken for a mosquito when flying. This tiny moth's wing span is smaller than 2 centimeters. It can be found throughout North America and in other parts of the world.

Millipede and centipedes have many legs. Too many to be called an insect, but we can still call them bugs. Legs can break off and be regrown!

The millipede shown here has curled up in a circle to defend itself. Millipedes have round bodies. Centipedes have flat bodies. A centipede has 1 pair of legs per body segment while a millipede has 2 pairs of legs per body segment.

Dung beetles eat poop!! They feast on the feces of animals that eat plants. Some of these plants are partially undigested. They eat other things too. The dung beetle is one of the few insects that raise their babies.

These beetles can be found feasting on poop on every continent except Antarctica. Not all dung beetles roll the dung, but those that do can move balls that weigh 50 times more than they do!

There are more kinds of insects than all other plant and animals combined! 80% of the animals on the Earth are insects.

Insects have been on Earth for a long time. A fossil of a cockroach has been found that is 280 million years old! The oldest insect fossil is estimated to be around 400 million years old. This was long before dinosaurs roomed the earth. An ancient dragonfly had a wing span up to 2.5 feet (0.88 meters). Can you imagine if this dragonfly was as big as a dog?

What do you think about insects and bugs? I like them!

So….

Did you learn new things about insects and bugs?

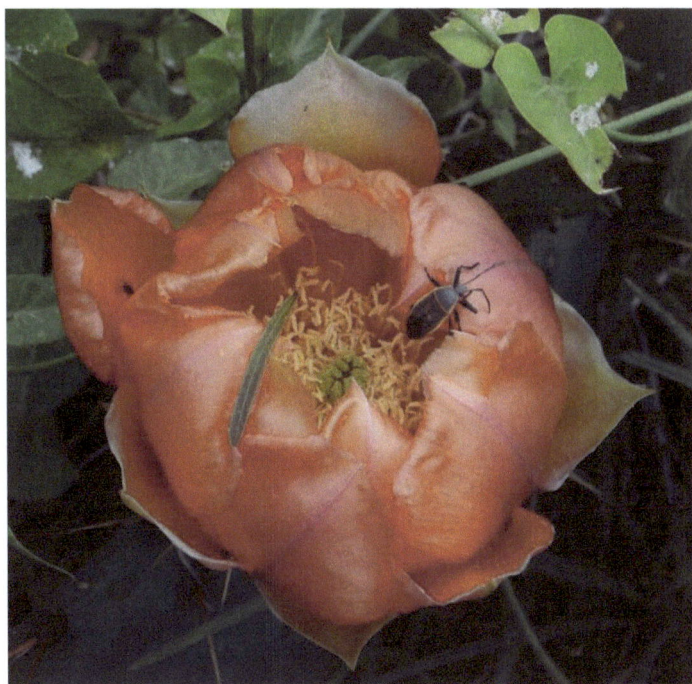

I hope you learned new things and enjoyed this book!

This is the fourth book in the series "So You Want to Learn About…" Please check out the other books in this series.

Thank you for reading.

Other books in this series

So You Want to Learn About Butterflies

So You Want to Learn About Reptiles & Amphibians

So You Want to Learn About Reptiles & Amphibia